Thinking Through The Fog

Willie Jamieson

BookLeaf Publishing

Presentation by *BookLeaf Publishing*

Web: www.bookleafpub.com

E-mail: info@bookleafpub.com

ISBN: 978-93-95755-81-8

First edition 2022

DEDICATION

This is dedicated to my friends who let me write about them, my mother who believed in me, and the journey I went on throughout this experience.

ACKNOWLEDGEMENT

This is to recognize my mother and friends as being motivation

PREFACE

Welcome to an attempt at, well something really.
It's been a while, I hope you enjoy

They Learn in Time

I have a friend named Rae
Who goes by them/they
"Too young," people say
"To know their way"

"Who I am, I have nothing to prove!"
"Fake friends and bigots is all I lose!"
"It's my choice, I so choose!"
"To be myself, and be not in the blues!"

Rae is an inspiration
Showing courage in this situation
Lost but found determination
To be themselves with no explanation

I am proud to be a friend of Rae
The courage and hope they display
Inspires me to be better everyday
You're doing amazing, okay?

Jumbled Thoughts Since The Day You Left

It took me two months to realize you're never
coming back to me
A concept I find hard to grasp when your
memory pops up
Ideally, I like the thought of you existing
peacefully, that seems to be, enters my mind
frequently
Simply to remind me of your continued
existence on your birthday, one of many you'll
never get to see
Why would the life I hate to live leave me in
misery without you
With you gone, I lost every connection to my
past self, which was never really reinforced of
course, but we knew it secretly
No chance to right the wrong, whatever
happened to in sickness and in health, you knew
me as well as myself, I guess it wasn't my right
to know
You lost your life, I lost a piece of my soul when
you breathed your last gasp of air, I swear it to
be so

I know you attempted to fight back as you
grasped to your fleeting sense of sanity as you
left this world behind
Not a day goes past where my thoughts don't
lapse to leave a message you'll never recieve just
to get it all out of my head
A message never to be read, like a letter in a
sinking ship that will never be sent, frozen in
time for all eternity
I don't write this to free me, of course I feel
guilty I couldn't save you, I miss you, I love you,
and I'm sorry
My teary eyes have never dried since the day
you died
I've tried and tried to get my thoughts down and
they just dance around since the topic is so taboo
It's okay to be not okay, I know I will be
someday, that much is always true
So I write this to the void as I can't avoid my
feelings and thoughts that wander back to where
you went
I love you
I miss you
Once again, I'm sorry
Please find yourself free to rest in paradise

You're In My Thoughts But I Don't Write About You Anymore, I'm Not Sorry

I remember when, I last wrote to you
It's been a month and a day, and a year or two
I'm still often wondering about how you do
Are you feeling better? Are you doing better? I
wish I knew

It's clear
That without you here
I'm doing just fine dear
But I'd be remiss if I didn't want you near

If it was wise to reach out I would
For now, I just write in stanzas hoping you're
good
I keep my distance as I should
Knowing I can't reach out even if I could

The thought of you settles in
Much to my chagrin
It's normal, because I been thinking
If I want to go through this again

My heart is closed
I'm indisposed
Due to the life I've chose
I'll make it picture perfect, so just strike a pose

I've been lost in thought
About you a lot
I try to pick up, but I'm at fault
While my thoughts continue to just assault

I'm on my last line
Like I said I'm fine
If only I could get you off my mind
I keep falling back in time to when you were
mine

Empty Thoughts

I feel lonely, although I am rarely alone. My thoughts tend to do a good job of reminiscing on times long gone, I tend to reread chapters of my life that ought to be left forgotten to time, I always seem to drift back into the quiet slumber of memories and nostalgia, and feel a twinge of pain in the past. More often then not, I swim through the channels of my swirling thoughts, pausing only long enough to see if I can pinpoint the moment I broke. As is with most things, the feelings subside, but the passion I feel in those fleeting moments of clarity remains instilled in my every essence. I feel whole for a brief second, perhaps a millisecond, or a nanosecond, or some non substantial unit of time measurement, yet I always return to where I was, not alone, but feeling lonely.

Stars Aren't Meant To Burn Forever Babe

The world was burning and all I wanted you to do was sit beside me as we watched it end. We accepted the fate of it long ago, it wasn't ours to save, but I was hoping for a paradise. Since time is fleeting, I tried to make one with you with whatever short terms of happiness I could grasp, I guess it wasn't enough. When the world blew up in our faces and everything was over, you walked away without a glance over your shoulder. It's fair that it settled to dust, I'm just sorry ashes are all that's left after it burned so bright

Things That Don't Matter Anymore

I would write you a poem
That you'd probably never see
So I will write myself a poem
For my own sanity

I would paint you a picture
Of your favourite view
I know it's not possible
To even get it to you

I would write you a song
You'd never hear me sing
I know you're not listening
So it doesn't mean anything

I would cross an ocean
Move a mountain across the earth
I know it doesn't matter to you
But it is what it's worth

I would do a lot for you
But you're not one to care
It's okay I'm fine
Even when you're not there

It's not possible for you
To see this and change your mind
It's all in memories now
Of when you were mine

Tides Change

Do you think the ocean craves the Moon? Constantly pulled in one direction and the next, changing depth to try and be closer to the Moon, bending, ebbing, flowing, trying to reach it. Do you think the ocean is aware of the storm it throws during its tantrums? Its ever raging typhoons, reaching towards the Heavens in a desperate attempt to reach what it is unable to touch, its hurricanes full of rage, visible from space, trying to make itself known to the Moon. Is the ocean insane, being in love with Luna, making it a lunatic? Maybe the ocean makes such violent storms to try and appease its love, knowing it will never have the ability to touch it, which in of itself is a tragedy. Love makes nature insane, even in nature. I wonder how the Moon feels about the oceans tears, and how the oceans cries out for the Moon in crashing waves, sunken ship, and empty waterline, day in and day out. I wonder if the ocean feels lonely, although it is full inside, it craves a touch it cannot feel in return.

I Found A Flower

I found a flower today
It reminded me of you
That's why I picked it
It reminded me of what could be
When it was us not just me
What could have been, should have been but
didnt
What I could of been was finally a "we"
I found a flower today
It was very beautiful
It made me think of you right away
It hurts when I think about you everyday
I found a flower today
It was just so pretty just like you
It was beautiful and perfect
Just like you always will be
In my eyes
I will always think of you when I see this flower
I found a flower today
I took a picture before it died
Too bad my love for you wont die anytime soon

The Closing Of A Chapter

When we were together
I wrote of flowers and oceans
Butterflies, kittens, and puppies
Everything that was beautiful in life

When you left me
I wrote of void, emptiness, and space
Destruction, devastation, and decay
I wrote how you made me feel

When I started healing
I wrote of rebuilding, growth, and spirit
I wrote of home, familiarity, comfort
I wrote about my journey

When I relapsed
I wrote of whisky, toxins, and poisons
Cannabis, cigars, and cigarettes
Anything to clear my mind of you

When I think of you now
I write of remembrance
Of passion and retrospect
Of days gone by, all to clear my mind

When I finally forgot about you
I didn't stop writing about your memory
I started to write again
And I simply forgot to remember to forget

A Fear Of Mine

I have a fear of drowning.
A fear in which no matter what I do, I always
see myself going under. The waves crashing
around me, myself struggling to get back up, but
no matter what, I can't seem to find ground to
stand on or get closer to the top. I always seem
to sink deeper and deeper until I hit bottom, and
even then, it's not over. On the bottom, it seeps
into my body, my lungs, my mind, my heart, my
very soul, being crushing while I'm drowning. I
kick, thrash, try all I can to get out of it, but it is
all in vain. No matter what, I drown and die.
The problem is, I'm not afraid to drown in the
water. It's depression that I'm scared of drowning
in, and I seem to fall deeper everyday, until one
day, I'll drown.

Some Drink

Some drink to remember
Some drink to forget
Some drink for celebration
Some drink for regret
Some drink to their health
Some drink to their grave
Some drink to be happy
Some drink to enrage
Some drink to be snooty
Some drink to fit in
Some drink to be kind
Some drink because they need a win
They choose to drink
Put poison in their veins
When life gets you down
Surely, some of you, do the same
Some drink to excess
Some drink to the floor
Some drink so much
They forget the night before
Some drink for addiction
Some drink for fun
Some only choose to drink
Simply because they are young
Some drink in silence

Some drink in pride
Some drink to kill
The feelings they have inside
Some drink about this
Some drink about that
Some drink for a person
They are never getting back
Some drink for circumstance
Some drink to feel alive
But something you should never do
Is ever drink and drive
Play it safe, be smart
Always do you
But don't get in the car
After too much brew
You have one life
Live it well
Drink a drink to drink a drink
But arrive home safely
 I care, can you tell?

I'm A Masterpiece With Or Without You

I'm a masterpiece
Although I lie, I'm incomplete
So what if I'm not finished
I'm my own artist
I'm my own place, my own sound
I fill in the blanks myself when no one is around
I'm not going to be able to be admired
I'm not sure if I'm desired
I'm what one calls original
I'm often times hard to control
I'm not one to make wishes
I'm sorry for my broken dishes
I'm required not to hated
But I sure make people frustrated
I'm a true piece of work
But I know my self worth

Empty Thoughts

I feel lonely, although I am rarely alone. My thoughts tend to do a good job of reminiscing on times long gone, I tend to reread chapters of my life that ought to be left forgotten to time, I always seem to drift back into the quiet slumber of memories and nostalgia, and feel a twinge of pain in the past. More often then not, I swim through the channels of my swirling thoughts, pausing only long enough to see if I can pinpoint the moment I broke. As is with most things, the feelings subside, but the passion I feel in those fleeting moments of clarity remains instilled in my every essence. I feel whole for a brief second, perhaps a millisecond, or a nanosecond, or some non substantial unit of time measurement, yet I always return to where I was, not alone, but feeling lonely.

Juilet And Her Bug

Juliet is in the bathroom
She's just a mosquito
Because anyone I've been Romeo
I've only been a bug to
I've been a pest
Fly around when necessary
Not having a care
Not necessarily
I yearn for life
More space in your garden, perhaps a bee
But a lowly bug
Is all I amount to be
A snug bug in a rug
Fly if I must
Only to buzz in your ear
With some semblance of trust
I've annoyed, amused, enthused
Every time I am near
Whether it says pfft
Or spring time is here
All I am is a simple
Simple little bug
Just looking for my garden
Garden of love

The Price Of Success

Though his memory was not lost
His achievements will soon be topped
His was a dream come true
But like all dreams, reality must be dropped

He was famous, this is the truth
His story was quite well known
To follow in his footsteps
To make a name all of their own

Is the dream he left
For all to follow
Although he may have died
The world felt no sorrow

A new king shall rise
The world will know his name
This young boy became a legend
Now its someone elses turn for fame

His last wish was to see
Someone else become
As big as he once was
They had to be number one

His lay in wait
Every night he would wait for news
He watched through rap, pop, hip hop
Rock, metal and blues

As he waited for the one day he knew
Someone would come to take his throne
His legacy he felt was on that would live
It would forever stand alone

As he lay in bed, waiting for his life to end
He turned to the news one last time
He found his successor was not a guitarist
But it was a person who could rhyme.

Old Habits Are Hard To Break

I used to write you anonymous poems, quite
often
Words of you would stain my arm like ink from
my pen
You'd penetrate my brain, tirelessly running me
over again
I've spent my fair amount of time putting words
onto paper like a lost friend
I wouldn't expect it to reach you, it was not a
piece on which I would depend
Everything finishes, everything must come to an
end
So I stand before myself, nothing left to defend
I'll start up a writing experiment, for more than a
weekend
I'll start and try to escape from this, a moment in
time I'll suspend
I'll write a bit a poetry, but I realize I'm just
writing anonymous poems to you again

I'm A Sailor

23

I'm a sailor
Lost at sea
Lost it seems
Is all I'll ever be

I'm a sailor
I have a ship
Leaky boat I live on
Barely survives a trip

I'm a sailor
I've tangled with a whale
Not Moby Dick
But still quite the tale

I'm a sailor
I tend to drink the rum
Drink it all
Until the bootle is done

I'm a sailor
My love is the moon
She lets me know
It'll all be safe soon

I'm a sailor
I drift from port to port
Never do I anchor
I am not that sort

I'm a sailor
Sometimes I decide to dock
Until I'm cast off again
To find another flock

I'm a sailor
I drift with the tides
Urning and churning
Like my insides

I'm a sailor
Loyal through and true
The only thing I am loyal to
Is the deep deep Blue

I'm a sailor
I've been through the storm
Been fighting all my life
Since I was born

I'm a sailor
I choose the life I live
But sailing all my life
Has left little of me to give

I'm a sailor
Broken, searching in the open
My little leaky ship
I hope it keeps on floating

Run Run Run

Do yourself a favour
And
Do what you've always done
What you've always done
Is
Just
Run run run
You fail to keep company
You fail to comply
You live
On the simple fact
Of
Just
Getting by
You attempt to fit in
To push and pull for
A place
Where no one quite
Recognizes
Just
A face
A place of passion
Of something
Much
More

A place you have never
Quite
Been before
A place of good bliss
A place
Not quite
Like this
So do yourself a favour
Do what you've always done
Run run run
For your
True place
Under the sun

For Her

One of my best friends there's every been
Is my friend Arlyn
Through thick and thin
I can count on them

The years have been long
They are so strong

Everything I've seen them overcome
It gives me confidence I'll find some

Of my own strength
To them I give thanks

While I am amazed they stay with me and give
me
The pleasure of their existence

It's been a ride no matter the distance
We're stuck together since the instance
We met
Can't separate us yet
Thanks for being here Arlyn!

Ashes To Ashes, Willie To Stardust

A friend I've know but never seen
Why that has at least 10 years it's been

Stardust is how she was known at first
Not her name given at birth
But the name she choose to show on this earth

She means a lot to me
Although I, Willie
Haven't met her personally
She's amazing and lovely

All of the good in this world
Must have been sent to this girl
If the the stars did twirl
In her direction they would swirl

She's beautiful inside and out
I couldn't imagine life without
She brightens my day with her name no doubt

From ashes to ashes, Willie To Stardust
I love you, with my soul I trust
Hope to be your friend forever
Nothing comes between us

The Moon

I go through phases
Just like the Moon

I change places
I hope to soon

I run races
All before noon

I make faces
When I use the wrong spoon

I'm a little complicated
It's just a bit of zoom

A bit of zap a bit of zip
My changes are just the tip

Take a seat
Enjoy the trip
I'm along for the ride of it